Bill Reynolds

MUSTANG

The Classic American Sportscar

Bill Reynolds

MUSTANG
The Classic American Sportscar

CRESCENT BOOKS
NEW YORK • AVENEL, NEW JERSEY

Featuring the photography of Nicky Wright

CLB 2981
© 1992 Colour Library Books Ltd., Godalming, Surrey, England
All rights reserved
This 1992 edition published by Crescent Books
distributed by Outlet Book Company, Inc.,
a Random House Company,
40 Engelhard Avenue, Avenel, New Jersey 07001
Printed and bound in Hong Kong
ISBN 0 517 07292 0
8 7 6 5 4 3 2 1

The Happy Accident

The birth of the Mustang was essentially a happy accident. Ford had successfully tried the "personal car" concept before, with the Thunderbird, and by the early 1960s these were already a legend, with people knocking on Ford's door asking why they couldn't repeat that success with something that looked sporty, handled better than the "land barges" of the day, and was affordable. What was more, the Chevy Corvair Monza was doing very well, despite its well-known handling deficiencies, and it was selling to a market segment for whom Ford had nothing – the very first of the Baby Boomers, then approaching car-buying age. The Corvette, also from Chevrolet, was a real American sports car that was selling strongly as well. And quite apart from domestic competition, about 80,000 people a year were buying imported sports (or at least sporting) cars. Ford was desperate.

A new car for this new market was inevitable, the only question was what it should be like. In retrospect, it is a miracle that they produced the legendary Mustang. The whole project could so easily have been a disaster, because there were two conflicting views inside Ford about what the new car should be. One camp wanted a "Corvette-eater" that would have 0-60 mph (almost 100 kph) in less than six seconds, independent rear suspension, disc brakes and serious handling. The other camp wanted a car which looked sporty, but which was really just a small, generic Ford, cosmetically cleaned up, sure, and with tauter handling than the Falcon and other current FoMoCo automobiles, but still a car with more style than real substance. One group wanted a two-seater, the other a four-seater. To cap it all, the "sporty" group was essentially pursuing the project as a "bootleg" exercise, working late after their regular assignments (and occasionally taking time off from them) to create the new car. Donald Frey was their leader, and they had no financial or other muscle inside the giant Ford bureaucracy.

The savior of the Mustang – for all that he was utterly and completely in the camp that favored "show" above "go" – turned out to be Lee Iacocca. When Frey's group presented him with a pretty body which he was sure he could sell, he repeatedly pushed top Ford management for the money to turn the ideas into a production car. And they did. At the New York World's Fair in April 1964, they introduced the "1964-1/2" Mustang – the odd model-year number is because, by tradition, "1964" models appeared in September 1963.

It certainly looked good. Although by modern standards it may look tall and boxy, with funny little thin tires, in 1964 it looked very sporting indeed when you stood it next to the heavy metal of the day. And if you ordered the right engine, it even went quickly or at least in a straight line. The biggest available engine was a 289 cid (4.7 liter) V-8 with 210 bhp SAE. For the only kind of performance that counted in America in those days, pure acceleration in a straight line, this was heady medicine, and 160 bhp/tonne was significantly greater than the new introduction from Porsche, the 911, which was only 120 bhp/tonne. Admittedly, the difference between SAE gross horsepower and DIN horsepower lessened the gap – SAE gross was measured with no engine ancillaries to sap power, and an effectively unrestricted exhaust, while DIN was closer to real-world "as installed" figures. But this was no slouch, with a top speed of close to 130 mph (well over 200 kph) and 0-60 mph times of eight-point-something seconds, and even the 260 cid (4.3 liter) engine delivered 164 bhp and a top speed of 115-120 mph (190 kph). Incidentally, the metric "tonne" has been used throughout this book when quoting power-to-weight ratios, because it is a useful compromise between the short ton (2000 lb) and the long ton (2240 lb), both of which are used without distinction in spelling in the England. A tonne is 2200 lb, or 1000 kg.

If you looked more closely at the details of the new Mustang, though, you soon saw that this was not altogether a purist's sports car. The large, heavy beam rear axle, with cart-type suspension, would hop and skip if pushed hard. A three-speed gearbox was not exactly state of the art. The nine-inch brake drums were incredibly puny, and would rapidly fade to almost nothing if you tried to drive quickly on a winding road. And at 27:1, the steering was more suited to a heavy limousine than to a sports car.

It didn't matter. Lee Iacocca had correctly surmised that the Mustang's superb good looks would gloss over any shortcomings. He also correctly predicted that many people would read the Road and Track test reports of the V8 fire-breathers, and be impressed. Although few of them would then go out and buy the "hot" Mustangs, many of them would probably buy the six-cylinder version anyway, because it was kinda neat. In the slang of the time, the Mustang was "bitchin' wheels."

With the straight six, it has to be admitted, the Mustang was not a very exciting motor car. The best you could say for its handling was that on a dry road it was almost impossible to summon enough power to get yourself into trouble, despite the archaic running gear. The 170 cid (2.8 liter) engine was never going to make 2,800 lb (1,273 kg) of car go very fast, certainly not 100 mph (160 kph), it just looked good, and it was cheap – $2,320.86, almost $2,000 cheaper than a Corvette.

At least, it was nearly $2000 cheaper than a Corvette *before* you started adding options, and the 1960s were the heyday of options. Adding the big V8, a four-speed transmission, the limited-slip differential, full instrumentation (the "Rally-Pac") and the "GT Equipment Group" (which was essential if you wanted any semblance of handling), meant that you also added about $800 to the bottom line. Then, given that the radio was another option (over $50), and that you could run through a whole list of other add-on goodies from "Deluxe Seatbelts" (at about $25) through the "Interior Decor Group" (over $100) to air conditioning (at $277.20), you could add another $500 without really trying. A cynic might almost have said that the marketing strategy was to sell the sizzle, with the steak as an option.

For the '65 model year (September 1964), the base six was upped to an even 200 cid (3.3 liters) and a nominal 120 bhp, which brought 100 mph in sight for even the humblest Mustang. It was hardly a performance engine, though, as the breathing was poor, and if you persisted in revving it to the limit in search of all 120 ponies, it was advisable not to do so for too long or you could break the whippy and ill-damped crankshaft.

The news on the V8 front was, however, more encouraging. As early as in June 1963, the biggest motor had been fitted with solid lifters in place of hydraulics, better breathing arrangements (including a big Autolite carburetor with a less restrictive air filter, and a dual exhaust), a higher compression ratio, and a general "beefing up" to give 271 bhp. With rather wider tires on 14-inch instead of 13-inch rims, there was a better chance of getting this power onto the road. Disc brakes, a $56.77 option, meant that there was a fair chance of stopping the beast and you could drag from 0-60 mph about a second faster than the previous generation – seven-point-something seconds. With any performance figures, of course, much depends on the state of the engine and how it has been cared for, the final drive ratio

(Mustangs offered plenty of options), and the skill and mechanical sympathy (or otherwise) of the driver. It was actually possible, by adding enough options, to bring the price of the car up to that of a Corvette, but most Mustangs were not sold in that type of trim. Then again, with the exception of Carroll Shelby's Cobras, most Mustangs could not take on a Corvette and win.

Carroll Shelby and the Cobra Legend

Carroll Shelby was the man who really created the Mustang's sporting image, despite Iacocca's assertion that racing didn't matter any more. It did, and without the Cobras the Mustang would probably never have achieved the legendary status that it enjoys almost worldwide today.

The Shelby Cobra GT350 began as a '65 Mustang fastback, with the 289 cid, 271 bhp engine and the four-speed box with limited-slip differential – the most powerful package available from Ford. Then the fun started.

The old Autolite and inlet manifolds were substituted with a high-rise inlet and a 700 cfm Holley, breathing through a functional air scoop in a specially-made, lightweight GRP hood. "Tri-Y" exhaust manifolds replaced the stock headers, and exhaled through glass-pack mufflers which exited just in front of the rear wheels, giving a real hot-rodder look, and sound. The stock oil pan (sump) and valve covers (rocker boxes) gave way to light alloy replacements, and not only did they look better, but oil capacity was increased, and the alloy sump contributed significantly to improved cooling. This took care of the basic power increase, to about 306 bhp, but still gave excellent reliability.

Next the suspension was sorted out, beginning with moving the stock upper control arm mounting points and adding a one-inch front stabilizer bar. To avoid front end flex, not one but two engine-compartment braces were added, which in turn permitted tighter steering, though it was still not rack and pinion. At the back end, over-the-axle traction bars helped to tame the lively beam axle, and although not as good as independent rear suspension, they were much better than the stock Mustang set-up. Koni shock absorbers helped, too. Disc front and drum rear brakes took care of stopping, and the rear drums were 10 x 2.5 inch, bigger and wider than normal. Kragar mag-alloy wheels reduced unsprung weight and put more rubber on the road.

The rear seats were pulled out and replaced with a much lighter and considerably neater GRP shelf, and the result was a dramatic two-seater that could run standing quarters in the 14 seconds, and go from 0-60 mph in under seven seconds. It also handled very much better than the stock car, partly as a result of the "added lightness," partly as a result of the suspension modifications, and partly because the battery was relocated to the trunk in order to make the car less nose-heavy.

The "GT350" side stripes came with the package, but, perhaps surprisingly, what we now regard as the trademark of the Cobra, the big front-to-rear, over-the-top stripe, was an option. Some Cobras were actually sold without this stripe, while the stripe itself was sometimes added by Shelby, sometimes by the dealer who sold the car, and sometimes by the buyer, and of course plenty of buyers put them on ordinary Mustangs, to get the Cobra look.

While this road-going Cobra was a car that could decently take on a Corvette – the de facto standard by which any American sports car had to be judged – there were still more radical Cobras which could actually beat Corvettes on the track. Admittedly, a racing Corvette was likely to be a much more civilized machine to drive, but the Mustang GT350R (for "Racing") was just more.

Engine power was upped to 350 bhp, albeit at the expense of smooth running and fuel economy. There was no way you were going to get a Cobra out of single-digit, miles-per-gallon figures, given that the stock 371 bhp machine was good for about 14 mpg (16 liters/100 km). To take care of the inevitable overheating that occurs when this sort of power is sustained, as it has to be for racing, Shelby added a higher-capacity radiator and an oil cooler, with liberal air-scoops for them and for both front and rear brakes.

More lightness was added by substituting Plexiglas for all save the windshield, and by having sliding side windows instead of wind-up, while 15 x seven-inch mag wheels increased your chances of avoiding wheelspin. A 32-gallon (116 liter) tank all but filled the trunk, was filled via a wide-mouth racing filler, and emptied by an electric pump which was less reliable than the standard mechanical pump, but could shift much more fuel per minute. A roll bar, over-the-shoulder racing harness, and stock fire extinguisher, all emphasized that this was a car to be driven very quickly indeed, without compromise. No fewer than 37 GT350R Mustangs were built, out of a total of only 562 Shelby Mustangs for 1965, an impressive six and a half per cent of the total.

Unfortunately, Ford did not see things Shelby's way. Even though the Mustang was selling like hot cakes, and though the Shelby Cobras had to be a contributing factor to those sales, the somewhat short-sighted accountants at corporate headquarters saw the Cobra as an inconveniently low-volume, low-profit car. They decided that if they made it more like other Fords, it would sell better.

The limited-slip diff and the Konis were made options instead of standard equipment, the exhausts were returned to the conventional out-the-back variety, the rear seats were left in, spring rates were softened, and the stock tin hood was used instead of the lightened plexiglass variety. Then, in the course of the 1966 model year, the suspension was reverted to little better than stock, with unmodified suspension mounting at the front, and under-the-axle traction bars in place of the original over-the-axle variety. This considerably poorer-handling car was, however, available with the option of a Paxton supercharger, for the traditional American ideal of a straight-line special.

Admittedly, the new Cobras did sell better – 2,380 cars, though a thousand of those were actually bought by Hertz as rental cars. But this immediately raises the question of whether the new Cobras sold because of their own virtues, or because of the promise of exclusivity, which had after all been generated by the '65 models. In other words, did the buyers for the '66 Cobras think they were getting a steak, but received only the sizzle, or was the sizzle all they wanted anyway?

For the following year, the Cobra was pretty much a standard Mustang with some extra GRP around the front end, little more than a top-of-the-line Mustang which was being used as a self-funding test bed for next year's styling. Admittedly, the news was not all bad, at least in the engine department. The 427 cid (7-liter) "homologation special" with forged crank, forged rods and pistons, and two 652 cfm Holleys, found its way into 47 of the '67 Mustangs, and with a nominal 425 bhp they were the most powerful Cobras ever built. These Super-Mustangs, and those fitted with the less potent but still dramatic 428 cid engine and 90 bhp less, were sold as the GT500. At this point, though, we have got ahead of ourselves, because we left the regular or "cooking" Mustangs at the beginning of the '66 model year, and the '67s were a different kettle of fish.

Beauty and the Beast

Not much happened to the Mustang for '66. The millionth Mustang was built – a pretty impressive trick for a car that was introduced late in the '65 model year. But apparent inertia was merely a mask for fast and furious redesigning at Ford, who had to bring their usual three-to-five-year new-model lead time down to a matter of *months*. The success of the Mustang had been even greater than they had hoped, but they knew full well that they had started a bandwagon rolling. It was obvious that GM would be going after the same market, and it was also fairly clear that GM's new cars would probably be even better looking, and almost certainly more powerful, than the Mustang. Thus, even though Ford would continue to peddle a vehicle propelled by the somewhat underwhelming 200 cid straight six, they knew that in order to stay in the limelight, they would have to come up with something new. The 1967 Mustangs would have to look better, and go faster.

Technically, the result was pretty much what anyone could have predicted – the new car was larger, heavier and more powerful. What was not so predictable, though, were the superb good looks of the new Mustang, especially the fastback. The elegant slope of the steeply-angled rear window was pure classicism, with the line dropping smoothly to the squared-off and slightly recessed tail. At the front end, the appearance of the slightly odd headlight layout was better from some angles than others. The expanse of painted metal between the outer lamp and the inner one, which was tucked into the hood proper, was not a total visual success from all directions, unlike the rear end.

The side-scoops were borrowed more or less equally from the Corvette and from Ford's own GT-40, which, despite Iacocca's disdain for racing, was creating serious credibility for Ford in Europe as well as in the United States. The concave rear end, and the "C-stripes" around the side-scoops, were also GT40 "styling cues."

Inside, the dashboard had been cleaned up considerably, with the instruments neatly deployed, unlike the somewhat haphazard arrangements of yesteryear. The interior decor option dropped the Galloping Ponies – they may be "classics" now, but at the time numerous people laughed at them – and the whole car was much prettier.

The convertible was the most expensive body option, with 25,738 made in 1967, but only 42,000 of the fastbacks produced, while the two-door hardtop, not as exciting but with the least expensive body style, sold over a quarter of a million. This is a recurrent theme in the whole Mustang story – very large numbers of the less exciting Mustangs sold on the strength of considerably fewer vehicles which were quite clearly classics. The "cooking" Mustangs were not bad cars, they were reliable, good-looking, and comfortable, but they lacked the glamour of the fastbacks, the convertibles, and the big-engined models.

You also have to remember that with a company the size of Ford, even "small" production figures are pretty impressive, and the 78,000 convertibles and fastbacks that they sold in 1967 would have been more than many small European makers could have made altogether.

To return to the mechanical side, the extra power was not all good news. The new top-of-the-line "big block" 350 cid (5.7 liter) engine was a large, heavy, rather old-fashioned motor which was not really suited for sporting use – two-bolt mains and hydraulic valve actuation do not immediately scream "performance." Worse still, the very tolerable 53/47 per cent front/rear weight distribution became 56/44, for a distinctly nose-heavy car.

Even so, the new big-block was powerful, which badly hurt sales of the considerably sweeter-handling 289 cid K-engine. Only 472 Mustangs were built in '67 with the K-motor, which makes them rather collectible, but then in '68 Ford rolled out the really powerful engines.

The first, already mentioned in connection with the GT500, was the 427 cid engine. As installed in a stock Mustang, it was downrated to only 390 bhp, and a single 650 cfm Holley, hydraulic valve actuation, and mild cam profiles, did not allow the engine to realize its full potential. Aftermarket tuners managed to extract well over 400 bhp reliably, and maybe 500 bhp in "whiz-bang" or "grenade" form. Astonishingly, this wonderful, race-bred engine was available only with a three-speed automatic box. It was, however, very short-lived, and was dropped in December 1967 after it had served its purpose of showing that it was a genuine production engine. There was then a hiatus for almost three months, until the 428 cid Cobra Jet motor came out.

The extra cubic inch took it over seven liters, which was neither here nor there except for racing, but the important thing was that it was significantly cheaper to produce than the 427 cid, being essentially a hotted-up version of Ford's standard big-block. When ordered as an option, the extra cost over the base engine was $434 instead of $622. The declared power of the motor was 335 bhp, though many suspected that this was for insurance purposes only, and that the true power was closer to 400 bhp. All this power still ran through a hippity-hop, solid rear axle, though the shock absorbers were staggered or angled one way on one side, the other way on the other, in an attempt to counter the torque reaction of the big beam, a solution which worked surprisingly well. Larger tires on six-inch rims were a help, though "laying rubber" was still all too easy with enthusiastic acceleration. A four-speed manual transmission was not merely available, but standard with this motor.

At the other end of the scale, the same old straight-six still powered the Mustangs for the masses, grinding out its nominal 120 bhp and, if you did not overtax it, proving very reliable. In between this and the 429 cid engine were assorted V-8 motors of 289 cid (4.7 liters) and 195 bhp, 302 cid (5 liter) and 210 or 230 bhp, and 390 cid (6.4 liters) and 325 bhp. What got interesting was when you started adding on the options.

The base model, with the six-cylinder engine and the two-door hard-top body, was listed at $2,578.60. Going for the convertible added $235.62, but let's assume you followed the fashion of the time and bought the fastback at $2,689.26. Add the 428 cid motor ($434.00), the four-speed manual transmission ($233.17), the required power disc brakes ($64.77), the GT Equipment Group ($146.71), the tachometer ($54.45), the limited-slip differential ($41.60), and the Wide Oval tires ($78.53), and the bill had already hit $3,742.49. This was for handling options alone.

Now suppose you added some creature comforts: power steering ($84.87), tinted windows ($30.25), air conditioning ($360.30), AM/FM radio ($181.39) and tape ($133.86), tilt-away steering wheel ($66.14), center console ($53.71), Interior Decor Group ($123.86), and a fold-down rear seat for easier luggage carrying ($64.77). You would now have added another $1,099.15 to the bill, for a spectacular total of $4,841.64 – no less than $2,263.04 over the base price! There would not be many options left that you didn't have, but you could just about hit $5,000 if you tried hard.

The whole question of options is a fascinating one, and it is worth noting that when the Japanese wiped the floor with the American automobile industry a couple of decades later, they offered very few options. The car came fully equipped to start with, and you didn't have to argue with the dealer about which options you wanted, and which ones he had in stock, and which ones you had to accept (at your expense!) in order to get the ones you were hoping for, which was always a source of friction. Did the American manufacturers spoil their customers for choice, were options a classic example of something which suited the trade, but not the customer? It's an intriguing, and probably unanswerable, issue.

The Boss

On February 6th, 1968, Semon E. "Bunkie" Knudsen left GM and became the boss at Ford at a $600,000-a-year salary. Although the restyle for the '69 models was already well under way, he and the other newcomer Larry Shinoda, were able to give the new Mustangs a sharp push in their own direction.

Shinoda was a stylist with a flair for marketing, and he was apparently responsible for the "Boss 302" name, as Ford's original intention had been to call it the "SR-2," which Shinoda aptly remarked was a poor imitation of the Z28 Camaro handle. Although some find his styling excessive, with more consideration for appearance than for function, he had a higher regard for engineering than most people at Ford, and he managed to persuade them that rear wings, front air dams and other such aerodynamic considerations warranted serious consideration. At the very modest speeds of which the base Mustangs were capable, all these things did was to add to the drag, but they did have two advantages. If the car had a powerful engine, they were genuinely functional, and even on the six-cylinder models, they looked functional.

The Boss, like the other models in the line-up, was essentially a re-skin of the previous year's model, with the same wheelbase of 108 inches (2743 mm), and a fractionally wider track of 0.4 inches (10 mm). But the body was almost an inch wider, close to two inches longer, and at least 150 lb heavier, giving a total weight of 3,300 lb (1500 kg). If that was not heavy enough, one option added a further 55 lb of sound-deadening material, and by the time all options had been installed, it was easy to exceed 3,500 lb (1591 kg). The side-scoops all but vanished, reduced to a vestige with a fake rear-brake cooler at the back, and "ordinary" would have been flattery for the two-door hard-top. The rear-end treatment of the fastback (now inexplicably renamed the SportsRoof) was determinedly modern, but lacked the elegance of the former version, while the front end just looked plain odd, an inferior version of what had gone before. The inside was slightly tacky, with plenty of plastic wood, though the optional boy-racer steering wheel added a touch of humor by being sold as the "Rim-Blow" option.

At the bottom end of the range, at $2,618.00, the same tired old straight six was expected to haul all this unaerodynamic metal around. Now rated at 115 bhp, it gave the base Mustang a searing 77 bhp/tonne at best, and quite possibly as little as 72 bhp/tonne. Incredibly, Ford upped this model to 250 cid (4 liters) by increasing the stroke to create an undersquare engine (the bore:stroke ratio was 0.94:1) but at least managed to extract 150 bhp from it in the process, restoring power-to-weight ratios to a respectable 100 bhp/tonne and bringing 100 mph back in sight.

But enough of such depressing news. At the other end of the spectrum, there was now a 429 cid engine, again just over the 7-liter mark (it actually displaced 7022 cc) and now equipped with a significantly oversquare configuration at a bore:stroke ratio of 1.21:1 (110.7 x 91.2 mm), compared with the old 428 cid engine which had been all but square at 104.9 x 101.1 mm. The new mill delivered a nominal 375 bhp, which may even have been an understatement. For comparison with the sixes, the Boss 429 offered a power-to-weight ratio of up to about 240 bhp/tonne, well over three times as much as the base model!

Like the former 427 cid motor, it was another "homologation special." Ford had to build at least 500 such motors to prove that it really was a production engine for NASCAR homologation. Alloy heads were the real news, along with monster valves (2.28 inch/57.9 mm inlet, 1.9 inch/48.3 mm exhaust), and when you look at these soup-plates, it is not hard to see why four-valve heads came in later! The besetting fault of the 429 was, however, poor lubrication, and unless it was heavily modified it used to run down its main bearings if the engine was kept at more than 6,000 rpm for any length of time.

Although the suspension was modified and the track widened, and despite other modifications such as relocating the battery in the trunk, the 429 was still something of a brute. In reality, the Boss 302 was a much better car,

even though the Boss 429 Mustangs, of which 899 were made, inevitably attract more attention.

The small-block engine of the 302 meant that overall weight and front/rear weight distribution were both more acceptable than with the larger motor, and there was no great shortage of power. While the stock 302 cid (5-liter) motor delivered 220 bhp, the Boss produced 290 bhp through the use of forged crankshaft and rods, four-bolt mains, solid lifters, and valves the size of soup-plates sucking through a 780 cfm Holley and blowing through twin exhausts. There was a functional front air dam – the rear aerofoil was an option, and of disputable value – and like the Boss 429 the suspension was "tweaked" significantly to improve handling. The only real drawback with the Boss 302 was that if you drove it too enthusiastically you could overcook the pistons, and they were known to crack as early as at 10,000 miles.

Aside from the options already mentioned – the two sixes, the two Boss Mustangs and the standard 302 – there was a total of five other engines also available in the 1969 model year, which seems a little excessive. Briefly, they were the 351 cid (5.7 liter) in two-barrel and four-barrel form for 250 bhp and 290 bhp, the 390 cid (6.4 liter) with 320 bhp, and two 428 cid engines rated at 335 bhp. Both 428 cid motors were available with the $84.25 "Shaker" scoop, which allowed a flap to open during full-throttle acceleration and feed the engine with lots of cool, if unfiltered, air, but the 428CJ-R had stronger connecting rods and an oil cooler. It also cost $133.43 more than its less sophisticated brother.

In 1970, the styling was somewhat improved by moving both pairs of headlights inside the grille area, and the "Shaker" scoop was available on all V-8 engines of 351 cid and above. This part got its name from the fact that it was mounted on the engine and stuck up through the hood, so that as the engine shook, so did the scoop.

End of an Era

The 1971 Mustangs were handsome but huge. The wheelbase grew yet another inch to 109 inches (2767 mm), the track by three inches (76 mm), the length by 2.1 inches (53 mm), and the width by 2.3 inches (58 mm). And they weighed about 3750 lb (1705 kg), about 850 lb (386 kg) more than the original 1964-1/2 cars.

As usual, the most handsome body was the fastback, a sculpture of huge, clean, smooth lines with refreshingly few gewgaws. The rear end was particularly fine-looking, with the rear window inclined at only 14 degrees from the horizontal. However, its very steep slope meant that it was all but impossible to see through the window unless it was sparkling clean, and as it had no rear wiper there was a considerable greenhouse effect which baked the interior of the car on hot summer days.

The two-door coupe, the mainstay of the line, had the same broad, bluff front, but the rear end was less successful. The "flying buttress" rear pillars concealing a conventionally-sloped rear window lacked conviction, especially when compared with the Jaguar XJ-S, the Lotus Europa, or various models of Italian exotica. And while the convertible had the inevitable charm of a ragtop, its styling could hardly be called inspired.

To make all this metal move, the top option was the 429SCJ-R (Super Cobra-Jet Ram-air) which was Ford's big block with solid push-rods instead of hydraulic valve actuation, as well as forged pistons and a Holley 780 cfm carburetor. In this form, you could have either the four-speed manual or the C-6 automatic, but you had to have either the Detroit Locker limited-slip diff ($207) or the Traction-Lok ($155) – the Drag Pack.

Or, of course, you could go to the Boss 351. Revised NASCAR rules meant that the 351 engine could be raced, and the new 351 Boss replaced the old 302 and 429. It came with solid lifters, forged connecting rods on specially-selected crankshafts with four-bolt mains, an 11:1 compression ratio, and a 750 cfm Motorcraft carb. Because it was the "small block" design, the weight distribution was significantly better than with the "big block," and this, together with the fairly lightly-modified suspension, meant that the Boss 351 was considerably better than the 429 at tricky maneuvers like cornering.

Because the 200 cid engine would have meant a power-to-weight ratio of under 70 bhp/tonne, it was finally dropped, and the 250 cid straight six became the base engine, with 145 bhp translated to 85-90 bhp/tonne, depending on the weight of accessories you ordered.

These bhp/tonne figures are interesting, because you might think that a car which could handle 330 bhp (Boss 351) or 375 bhp (429SCJ-R), for 195 bhp/tonne and 221 bhp/tonne respectively, would be easily able to tame 90 bhp/tonne. Except, of course, that without extensive suspension modifications, the Mustang was not fully able to handle the big motors, and rather than being a car that

was designed for the big engines, with smaller options available, it was essentially a car that was designed for the smaller engines, with bigger options available. This was why it looked like, and in many ways was, such good value. For the unskilled driver who wanted blinding acceleration, the big-engined Mustangs were ideal, but anyone who tried to sling them around corners would soon find that the big ponies were somewhat lacking in traction, brakes, and a number of other desirable handling characteristics. Ordering the "competition" or "handling" options – which were in any case required with the most powerful engines – improved matters immensely, and the Boss 351 was better still. But not until you started modifying the suspension significantly, instead of just stiffening it, were you going to get a car which was competitive. Iacocca had summed it up almost a decade earlier when he said that Ford was not out to build a car for real sports-car buffs, because the market was not big enough. The Mustang aimed for a much larger constituency, and found it.

To return to the engine options, though, the others were three less powerful versions of the 351 cid motor, all the way down to 240 bhp, and a 210 bhp version of the 310 cid V-8. This meant that there was one six and three sizes (and six or seven power outputs) of V-8. Cosmetic "Mach 1" graphics, Boss side-stripes and other accessories were made available even if you ordered the six-cylinder motor, so some of these mean-and-magnificent-looking Mustangs were real sheep in wolves' clothing, and with the base engine option, they could barely stumble out of their own way.

For 1972, there were no body changes and the two most dramatic engines disappeared: the big-blocks and the Boss 351. In response to forthcoming government legislation, engines were downrated to run on "regular" gas instead of the high-octane petrol which was on the way out. To obscure the nature of the change, though, power outputs were quoted in SAE net instead of SAE gross, in other words, "real world" power instead of "test bed" power. SAE net is comparable to, or lower than, DIN bhp.

The base six dropped to 98 bhp, the two-barrel 302 dropped to 140 bhp, the two-barrel 351C to 177 bhp, and the four-barrel 351CJ to 266 bhp. The interesting thing is that all this down-rating came just before the so-called Gas Crisis, so the American muscle car was already on the wane when OPEC put the squeeze on the oil importing nations. A conspiracy theorist might be very tempted to argue that the "gas crisis" was actually a plot by the CIA, the Military-Industrial Complex, or someone similar, in order to promote the U.S. government's new fuel policies!

Be such fantasies as they may, the most powerful engine in the 1972 line-up, and a very desirable one, was the 351 HO ("High Output") with 275 bhp SAE net. This was almost certainly over 300 bhp under the old "gross" rating, and it gave the Mustang 0-60 mph times in the sixes. Only about 1,000 cars with this motor were built, in all three body styles, and if you ordered this option, you also had to have power front discs, the Competition suspension package, and a four-speed manual gearbox feeding the power to wide tires on 15-inch wheels via a limited-slip differential. It was the last of the old-style performance Mustangs.

It seemed, though, that Ford was losing interest in the Mustang. This impression was only accentuated by the '73 models, where the only significant styling change was the rather well-executed color-keyed front bumper which had to withstand a five mph (8 kph) collision without damage. Engine power continued to drop, with the disappearance of the 351 HO, and the very fastest 1973 Mustang available could not accelerate as fast as a '65 with the 289 cid engine. Sales were waning – fewer than half as many Mustangs were made in 1973 as in 1968, and the 1968 figure of 317,404 was only about half as good as the 607,568 Mustangs of 1966. Not only was the old order changing, it had to be further changed, and quickly, if the Mustang was not to wither and die altogether. It was time for the Mustang II.

The Wilderness Years

The new Mustang was, in a sense, a "back to basics" motor car. Iacocca decreed that the new car should be lighter, sportier, more in the spirit of the original Mustang. He also decreed that "the convertible is dead and can be forgotten." But then we all make mistakes.

The wheelbase dropped by 12.8 inches (325 mm) to 96.2 inches (2443 mm), the track was narrowed by almost six inches (150 mm), and the width dropped by two inches (51 mm). The overall length came down to 175 inches (4445 mm) to make this the shortest Mustang ever, no less than 14.5 inches (368 mm) shorter than the previous year's models. And the whole car lost weight

drastically – over 1,000 lb (about 475 kg) to 2,700 lb (about 1225 kg). The only dimension which was not much decreased was the height, which was a mere 0.2 inches (5 mm) lower than its predecessor.

Rack and pinion steering was introduced to improve handling, especially for better cornering, and disc brakes were standardized on the front. Ford dropped the unbelievably primitive three-speed "crash" box as the base option, and replaced it with a four-speed, all-synchromesh unit.

So far, so good, but the bad news lay under the hood. Only two engines were available, a brand-new, all-metric 140 cid (2.3 liter) four-cylinder and the established European 171 cid (2.8 liter) V-6.

The four was the worst of all worlds, delivering a mere 88 bhp – an appalling 38 bhp/liter. The engine was too big to run smoothly, because about 1600 cc (98 cid), or at most two liters (122 cid), is as large as you can make a four without either running into severe vibration problems or using a balance shaft. Without a balance shaft, Ford was forced to mount the engine on plenty of rubber in the unitary chassis in order to isolate the driver from the worst of the vibration. With this engine, the new Mustang offered 0-60 times of 15 seconds and a top speed a fraction over 100 mph.

The V-6 was not much better. Sure, it was smoother, but its 105 bhp represented an indifferent 40 bhp/liter, and at best your Mustang would just about reach 85 bhp/tonne. At least the 100 mph barrier was easily exceeded, though not by a great deal.

The engines may have been a disaster, but the styling was not particularly clever either. The long hood/short deck theme was maintained within the limits imposed by the reduction in overall length. The fastback looked like a slightly pumped-up Ford/Mercury Capri, and the two-door coupe was as uninspired as it could possibly get. Ghia labels were cynically slapped on this undistinguished metalwork to create the "luxury" version (Ford had acquired Ghia in 1970).

As with the original Mustang, though for completely different reasons, the new Ford Mustang II still proved to be the right car in the right place at the right time. It arrived at the same time as the so-called "gas crisis," and public hysteria at the increase in gasoline prices, which still looked cheap to the rest of the world, meant that almost any reasonably economical car could be relied upon to sell like hot cakes. In its first year the Mustang

II sold over 385,000 cars – more than three times as many as in the worst year for the original Mustang, 1972, when only 125,093 were shipped.

In 1974 the 302 cid V-8 reappeared as a born-again Mach 1, but was only rated at 140 bhp, a staggeringly poor 28 bhp/liter. What was worse, it was only available with an automatic gearbox. The large engine and the automatic box added almost 600 lb to the base weight of the car, bringing it up to 3,290 lb (1495 kg), so the power-to-weight ratio was a miserable 94 bhp/tonne. The 0-60 times, at about 10 seconds, were about half as good as the earliest "Muscle Mustangs" – though the front/rear weight balance was so bad, at close to 60/40 per cent, that if the engine had been much more powerful, the handling might well have proved lethal. For comparison on bhp/liter figures, roadgoing motorcycles had already exceeded 100 bhp/liter, and the contemporary Ferrari GT4 BB flat-twelve delivered 82 bhp/liter, while at their height, Ford's own crude old all-iron V-8s had easily exceeded 50 bhp/liter.

But performance, as we have seen, was not where it was at. In 1975, for example, the Ghia acquired not only a vinyl half-roof, but also "opera windows" – two of the nastiest styling cliches of the period. At least "opera windows" were appropriate to a "crushed-cranberry-red velour" interior, which looked very like the interior of an 1890s opera box. Then in 1976, new depths of perfidy were plumbed by resuscitating the Cobra name as a purely cosmetic package – though if you wanted a Cobra, you did have to buy the V-6 or V-8 engine.

The 1977 model year saw another '70s cliche, the "T-Top," with two removable panels and a central "spine" between the rear window frame and the windshield – much more rigid than a true convertible, but also much less fun. Then in 1978 there was the "King Cobra" package, which gave you stiffened suspension and light alloy wheels, along with the cosmetics, but cost an expensive $1,277.

After the initial success, which had been mainly the result of Gas Crisis hysteria, sales of the Mustang II dropped significantly, and after the 385,993 cars of 1974, production never again rose above 200,000 a year, and in 1977 they were as low as 153,173. The Mustang II was not a complete failure, but nor was it anything like a complete success. As with the end of the previous generation, something had to be done quickly to increase the Musang's popularity.

Getting Back on Track

The new 1979 models reverted to the plain old "Mustang" name – maybe Ford hoped to recapture the old Mustang magic with the original name.

The styling of the first of the new Mustangs was still pretty generic, and very much of its time, but all kinds of practical improvements were made. The drag coefficient (Cd) came down to 0.44, which was not exactly state of the art – European production cars had already cracked the 0.40 barrier, and were looking for 0.35 or better – but which was markedly better than the Mustang II. To improve matters still further, the weight dropped by a significant 200 lb or so, despite the fact that the car became significantly longer and roomier. Wheelbase rose 4.2 inches (107 mm) to 100.4 inches (2550 mm), and overall length rose 4.1 inches (104 mm) to 179.1 inches (4549 mm). The car was made 1.1 inches (28 mm) narrower, but 1.6 inches (41 mm) taller. This made for a much more comfortable and all-round better car, with more room, a smoother ride, and improved fuel economy. Less weight and a better Cd may not have been the old-fashioned American Way, which relied on a bigger engine and regarded both weight-reduction and aerodynamics as something that happened to other people, but you could not argue with the numbers.

The new Mustang also handled better, thanks to McPherson struts at the front – Ford in Europe had used McPherson struts successfully for years - and a coil-spring rear end with four-link axle location. Steering remained rack and pinion, while brakes were disc front/drum rear, probably the best practical design for all but the most sporting cars.

The engines remained a problem, though. The base engine was the 2.3 liter all-metric four, still with 88 bhp, and the reduced weight of the car meant that this gave almost 70 bhp/tonne, which may not have been exactly sporty but which was still pleasantly driveable. The 2.8 liter V6 was the next step up, now with 109 bhp for just over 80 bhp/tonne, but in the middle of the model year it was replaced with the ancient 200 cid straight six – though this was now called a "3.3 liter" as America started to come to grips both with metrication. This geriatric motor was now rated at 85 bhp SAE net, or three bhp less than the 2.3 liter four, despite being considerably larger and heavier. It was, however, smoother, and it could tolerate even the worst abuse and lack of maintenance, which the four could not. Also, its extra torque allowed for quite economical gearing.

There were two ways of getting more power. One was to buy the 302 cid engine, now renamed "5.0 liter" and offering the same 140 bhp as the previous model year, and the other was to buy the turbocharged 2.3 liter four, rated at 132 bhp. While 57 bhp/liter is nothing too remarkable for a turbocharged engine, neither is it particularly poor for an oversized in-line four. But, for comparison, the 1975 Porsche 911 Turbo delivered 260 bhp from a turbocharged three-liter flat-six, some 87 bhp/liter, and the Porsche weighed about the same as the four-cylinder Mustang.

The weight saving of the four versus the eight meant that the power-to-weight ratio was much the same for both cars, and of course the turbo four was much nimbler, and for fast driving on winding roads, with generous use of the gearbox, it was a very much better car to drive. On the other hand, it lacked the famous low-speed "grunt" of the V-8 which, after all, offered more than twice the capacity. Consequently, it was not much use for drag racing (a crude but popular measure of performance), and it suffered from all the drawbacks that bedeviled first-generation turbos. Reliability was marginal to start with, and without proper maintenance it became very poor indeed. Also, it suffered from turbo lag. In other words, when you put your foot down, it took a little while for the turbocharger to catch up with the engine. When it did catch up, you got "shove-in-the-back" acceleration, but by that time, road conditions might have changed, so you would brake and find yourself accelerating and braking at the same time. Buyers must surely have agreed with W.O. Bentley's famous dictum that "Supercharging is a perversion of design. If you want more power, build a bigger engine."

The 302 cid V8 therefore remained the engine of choice, for all that it could provoke severe axle tramp even with only 140 bhp and for all that it made cornering much more interesting.

In 1979, the Mustang was chosen as the official pace car for the Indianapolis 500, and no fewer than 11,000 "replicas" were built. In fact, they were not true replicas at all, because the actual pace cars had somewhat special V-8s, while the "replicas" came with either the standard V-8 or the turbo four. The most striking thing about this T-top car was the graphics – galloping ponies in fading shades of gray, "OFFICIAL PACE CAR" in large red letters, "83rd Annual Indianapolis 500 Mile Race May 27th 1979" marked on the car, and a winged wheel. The interesting thing is that the cars were supplied in pewter and black, with red stripes, but the ponies and the text were supplied separately, to be applied by the dealer or even the customer. Very few cars, therefore, carried the full text, and indeed many even omitted the "OFFICIAL PACE CAR," while there were those who felt that even the galloping ponies might make the car too conspicuous.

For the third time, the first year of the new model boded success. Ford sold 369,936 cars, and they changed the model very little for 1980. The base four and the straight six both gained a few horsepower – 90 bhp for the four, 91 or 95 bhp for the six, depending on whether it was ordered with a stick-shift or the automatic transmission. However, the bore of the V-8 was reduced from four inches to 3.68 inches (101.6 mm to 93.47 mm) for a capacity of 4.2 liters and an output of a mere 119 bhp. What was more, the V-8 came only with an automatic gearbox.

The enthusiast was therefore left to contemplate the turbo four, which still offered 132 bhp and which could now be ordered with a new five-speed manual overdrive transmission. Unfortunately, the turbo had all the same drawbacks as before and, as a result, Mustang sales fell significantly in 1980 to 271,322, a drop of 98,614 cars, or almost 27 per cent.

The Turbo was deleted for the 1981 model year, though there was briefly another kind of Turbo – the McLaren Mustang. This was something like the old Cobra, in that the hottest Mustang in the line-up was "race-prepped," with increased engine power and all types of suspension and other modifications. It was the kind of car which might have attracted very favorable attention if it had come from some small, obscure Italian maker, but which hadn't a hope of selling at $25,000 with the Ford name on it. Besides, this was about twice the price of a contemporary Corvette.

At this point, the car which would eventually become the Probe must have seemed like the natural replacement for the Mustang – a very much more modern design and generally improved, with much lower drag, lower weight, and better handling. The 1982 Mustangs must surely have been seen as a stopgap, which shows how wrong you can be . . .

The Car that Wouldn't Die

The 5.0 liter came back for '82, now in H.O. (High Output) guise with 157 bhp. It was only available with the four-speed manual 'box, limited slip diff, power brakes and power steering, and a "handling package" which made the suspension significantly more responsive. At long last, the Mustang had again broken the 100 bhp/tonne barrier.

Bodywork changes were not very great – at least, not to the non-aficionado – though there was a certain amount of "cleaning up" of details, and with the exception of the new motor, there was nothing very remarkable about the '82 models. The most important thing, though, was that the return to performance signaled a change of emphasis.

In 1983, the wind of change reached gale force. The V-8 rose to 175 bhp (and the weight stayed under 3,100 lb, little more than 1400 kg), and two new engine options appeared. One was a revised Turbo, now rated at 145 bhp as well as being vastly more reliable than the original, it made for a most entertaining automobile. The other was an all-new 2.8 liter V-6, with alloy heads and rated at 112 bhp. This was an ideal "middle-of-the-road" Mustang, for someone who did not feel the need for serious power but who wanted a pleasantly quick, responsive, smooth car.

Best of all, 1983 also saw the return of the convertible. Like all convertibles, it was noisier, heavier, slower, more cramped and more expensive than a hard-top version of the same car. It was not even at the cutting edge of convertible technology, and it leaked, in quite vintage fashion, in anything more than light rain. It was, however, a proper American convertible, with a glass rear window in the power roof, and it looked just like a Mustang was supposed to look like – instant fun. Until part way through the 1984 model year, the convertibles were built by Cars and Concepts, an outside contractor.

Even with the new motor and the renewed allure of the convertible, sales were very poor. Fewer than 121,000 Mustangs were built in 1983: 33,201 sedans, 23,438 convertibles, and 64,234 three-door hatchbacks. But Ford persisted, and offered performance fans even more for 1984.

The four was available in normally-aspirated form, in basic Turbo form with 145 bhp, and in SVO ("Special Vehicle Operations") form with no less than 175 bhp, running a full one-atmosphere boost. The SVO was also equipped with Koni shocks at the front, "Quadra-Shocks" (two shock absorbers each side) on the back to help keep the rear axle in its place, bucket seats, 16-inch wheels with seven-inch rims, and a fair amount of functional aerodynamics, cooling scoops, and so forth. In many ways, the SVO with the turbo motor is the ultimate Mustang – Boss and even Cobras notwithstanding – because it can be thrown around a twisting road with considerably more aplomb than any other production Mustang before or since. And there were no worries about brake fade, as disc brakes were standard on all four wheels.

On the other hand, the SVO was significantly slower than the V-8 on the drag strip, required considerably more careful maintenance, and, worst of all, was much more expensive at $15,585. You could still buy a five-liter GT for under $10,000, and very few people were willing to spend close to six grand extra for a car which was far more suited to European conditions than to America's wide, straight roads, low speed limits, and vigilant speed cops.

You could now order the V-8 with either the five-speed manual gearbox or the four-speed automatic, but if you ordered the automatic you rather unexpectedly got a fuel injected engine which, even more unexpectedly, was *less* powerful than the carburetor version, at 165 bhp instead of 175 bhp.

And, of course, there was still the 2.8 liter V-6, but this time they had used the fuel injection to good purpose, to boost the power slightly. In this form, it delivered 120 bhp, 43 bhp/liter, and one more horsepower overall than the older 4.2 liter V8.

Despite all this, and despite the fact that it was the twentieth anniversary of the Mustang, sales were still poor. Fewer than 150,000 cars were built in 1984, including 5,260 20th Anniversary Specials. The Special package was purely cosmetic, consisting of white paint and a red interior with two 20th Anniversary dash plaques, but it was applied to 3,333 5.0L GTs and 120 5.0L Convertibles, 350 Turbo GTs and 104 Convertible Turbo GTs, plus 15 "VIP" convertibles and 245 cars from Ford of Canada. Not all cars had the second dash plaque installed, as after the car was sold, the plaque was supposed to be returned to Ford for engraving with the owner's name, and registration on a sort of "honor roll." It was a nice idea, but not everybody bothered, and some of those who did bother to fit them also bothered to remove them again when they sold the car, to have for a keepsake.

In 1985 the front end was changed to a rather dull slope, reminiscent of an old Volvo, but both power and handling were made more abundantly available for those whose tastes ran that way. The five-liter engine was upped to 210 bhp. There was nothing particularly novel about the cam changes, including the adoption of roller cam followers, or the new stainless-steel exhaust manifolds, but a revised accessory drive system was very clever. Except when idle, the alternator, power steering pump, and air-conditioner pump were driven at half engine speed, with consequent benefits in both top-end engine power and the longevity of accessories. The excellence and originality of this approach cannot be overemphasized, as any modern designer must look at ways to stop wasting power, which is precisely what this does.

The SVO was also pumped up to 205 bhp, with extra turbo boost, better breathing, bigger injectors and a hotter cam. The handling was also made more taut and responsive, and the ride was improved – stabilizer bar bushings were Teflon lined, and the engine was rubber mounted for greater passenger comfort. With a very much better front/rear weight distribution than the V-8, well under 3,000 lb (maybe 1350 kg), and only five bhp less than the V-8, the SVO offered better than 150 bhp/ton in a superb-handling package costing $14,806. The power was up to almost 90 bhp/liter, too, which is very different from the comparison figures which were given earlier. Now the Ford was in Porsche territory for specific power outputs, an impressive achievement indeed with the large, lumpy four.

Someone in FoMoCo must really have believed in the Turbo SVO, because the 1986 model year saw the V-8 switched to sequential port fuel injection at the expense of 10 bhp. This meant that the four-cylinder turbo SVO now had five more bhp than the V8, and was well over 100 lb lighter. Alas, in 1987 the SVO was finally dropped, but the V-8 was brought back up to 225 bhp, for 0-60 mph times in the six-second range and a 14-second standing quarter. This new-era Muscle Car also featured a re-styled front and rear which looked much better than the previous generation, and this is pretty much where the Mustang has stayed since.

Sure, the absolute power output of the current V-8s is significantly lower than it was in the great Muscle Car days, but 225 bhp SAE net in the new Mustangs probably equates to close to 300 bhp in the old SAE gross system, and the cars are lighter, more aerodynamic, better braked, and much better at turning corners. Several parts from the SVO found their way onto the V-8: a bigger stabilizer, bigger discs, really excellent seats, plus more. The drag coefficient of the GT is down to 0.36 for the GT, and even the sedan is 0.40, so high-speed cruising is better and so is fuel economy. A Ferrari it still isn't, but it is a lot cheaper than a Corvette, and unless you are a seriously fast driver it is all you could reasonably ask for. Since 1988, however, if you don't want the V-8 your only other choice is the old 2.3 liter engine in unblown trim – the V-6 was deleted.

At last, Ford had got the balance of the Mustang, with just the right combination of "go" and "show." In 1988, they sold more than 200,000 cars, and since then they have not looked back. There have been detail changes, such as 16-inch wheels with lower-profile tires on the V-8 (the four stuck with 14-inch wheels), and even an increase to 105 bhp for the four-cylinder, achieved via a higher compression ratio which necessitated twin-plugging the heads. But, altogether the car is astonishingly little changed from that 1987 turning point. There are now air-bags and so on and so forth, but essentially, the Mustang today has reverted to what the Mustang was in 1964 – front-engine, rear-drive, and fun. To anyone who says "Why don't they don't build 'em like they used to," the Mustang is a wonderful answer. In theory, it should have been replaced by the Probe, in practice, it's still here. It is the car that refuses to die.

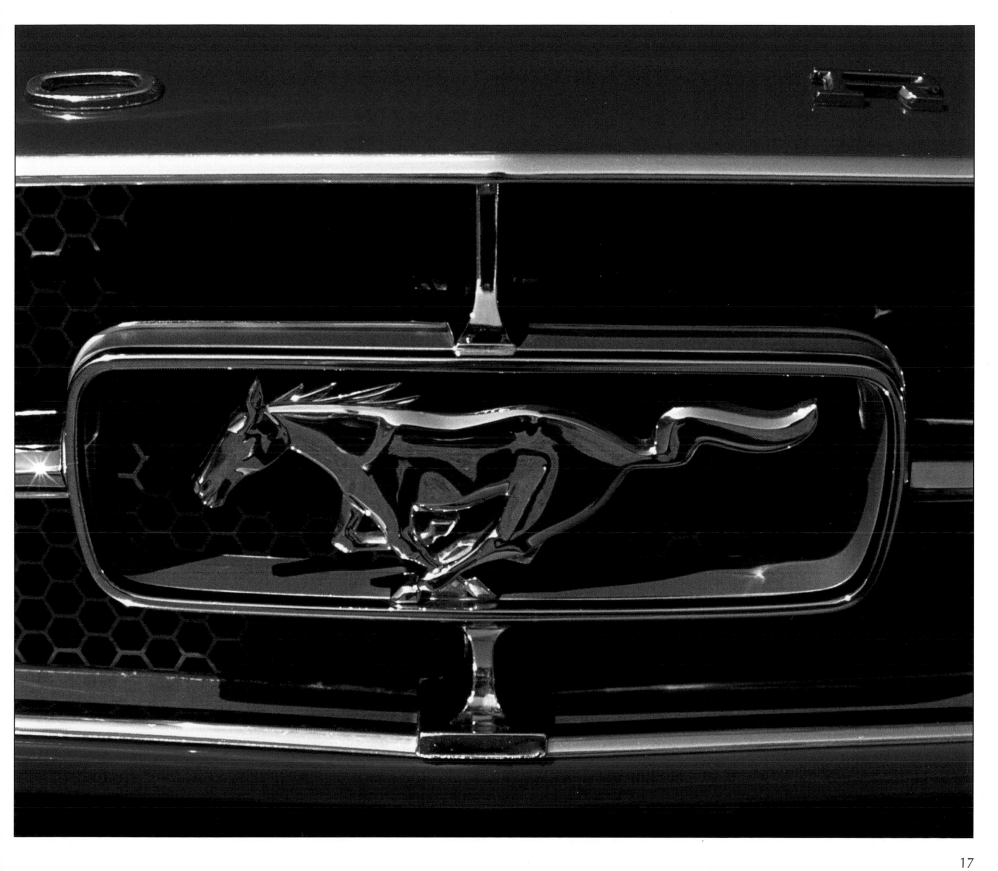

The new "Personal Car" from Ford was the logical successor to the early Thunderbirds – in fact, "T-Bird II" and "Thunderbird II" were considered as possible names before "Mustang" was chosen. With the V8 engine, the new baby Ford went as fast as it looked, too.

John Conley from Ford's advertising agency summed up the new name: "Mustang had the excitement of wide-open spaces and it was American as hell!" The three-box sedan was smart, but the convertible was even prettier – and while the V8 might call for extensive bracing of the engine compartment, it certainly provided a great deal of "go" to match the "show," while the straight-six was simple, economical, and reliable for everyday motoring.

If you look very closely at the Mustang, it is a triumph of design. There is no single feature that is individually new; there are no wild exaggerations of styling, and there are certainly no extravagances such as dual headlights. It is a car that is unmistakably built to a price – which makes the integration and originality all the more remarkable: the whole is significantly greater than the sum of the parts. If it still looks good today, consider what it was like when it first came out!

One of the great attractions of the Mustang is that it is quintessentially American. This early convertible just looks perfectly right in any setting: town or country, city or village, in a field of wildflowers, or with rugged hills in the background. The original Mustang was the American Dream in sheet metal with a motor; and for the most part, the styling was wonderfully clean and devoid of the gew-gaws that had so recently characterized American cars.

Choosing the right color often makes a great difference to how a Mustang looks – and you have never been able to go far wrong with red and white (or red and cream). The white top and the white "go-faster" stripe seem to "stretch" the car and make it longer, leaner, more aggressive. The discreet "289" badge is a word to the wise; then under the hood, all is revealed. The words "COBRA – Powered by Ford" are all you need to know... The same car appears overleaf.

One of the great attractions of the Mustang was that it looked right in almost any setting. Most cars photographed with a horseman in the background would look like a contrived, ad-man's fantasy. Mustangs – these are 1966 convertibles – look completely at home. The same goes for the gravel road. With most sports-cars, you would worry about the ground clearance, but the Mustang has a classic, vintage quality to it. The straight-six was arguably a better choice than the V8 if you were buying a convertible.

Inevitably, the open body was less rigid than the closed models, and wind noise was much greater, so there was less incentive to try to get the ultimate out of the engine. Power, however, was more than adequate for truly enjoyable wind-in-the-hair motoring, and sixes are much cheaper today than the larger-engined cars. On the other hand, most people who could afford a convertible when they were new could also afford a V8, so straight-six convertibles are not as common as they might be.

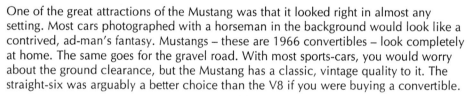

The 1966 Mustang Sprint 200 was a cosmetic pack available only with the 200 cid six: it featured wire wheel covers, pin stripes, a center console and a chrome air cleaner. Most cars ordered with the Sprint 200 option were hardtops; this Springtime Yellow convertible is fairly unusual. Note the omission of the fake rear brake cooling scoops, and the cleaner line that the car has as a result.

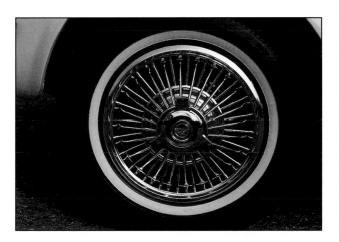

The "floating" horse in the air intake distinguished the 1966 Mustangs from the 1965s. There were other subtle differences, too: a bright molding on the hood lip, bright rocker panel moldings, and a redesigned gas cap. To the "collector," the very first Mustangs are worth significantly more than the 1966 cars, but to someone who wants a car to drive and to enjoy, a 1966 is likely to prove very much better value. Besides, who except a Mustang aficionado can tell them apart?

The new five-dial instrument cluster was both more attractive and more functional than its predecessor, but the three-speed manual transmission of the base model was beginning to look a bit old-fashioned by 1966; it was only the big, lazy engines of the period, essentially holdovers from the 1950s (and earlier!) that allowed such casual cog-swapping. Today, with "peaky" small engines delivering maximum power over a limited range of engine speeds, four- and better still five-speed 'boxes are essential.

The Shelby GT350 was the first, and in the opinion of many the greatest, of the Shelby-modified cars that bore the Cobra name. It was most assuredly not a tractable road machine: in effect, it was a racer that had been more-or-less tamed and made street legal. It took skill to drive it to the limit, but unless you drove it to the limit, there was no point in having it. The early Cobras were not cars for poseurs: they were noisy, thirsty, uncompromising, and very, very quick. Even the late 1966 cars were not as blatantly racers as the 65s and early 66s; this is a 1966, and may or may not have the relocated suspension that characterized the ultimate Cobras.

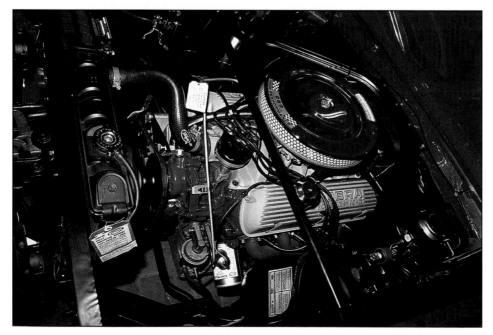

The "H" in "GT350H" stood for Hertz, who ordered a thousand GT350s. They were very much "softer" than the original fire-breathers: the engine was still very powerful, but the suspension was not fully modified. Most GT350H models were supplied with the three-speed automatic 'box. The rear scoops are functional, though.

The 1967 GT500 was very powerful – the 428 cid V8, based on the Police Interceptor engine, delivered 355 bhp. A few cars were even fitted with the 425 bhp 427 cid engine. The big block motors meant, though, that the car was not as well balanced as the GT350, even if it was very fast in a straight line.

Rather than being an out-and-out racer like the original GT350, the 1967 GT500 was more of a flagship Mustang and a test-bed for new styling ideas – including non-functional rear scoops. The nose was extended three inches with GRP, while the rear deck lid was provided with a prominent spoiler. The GRP hood was unique to this model, and the scoop actually was functional. On most cars, the big driving lights were in the middle, as shown here, but for some states they were moved out beside the headlamps in order to meet construction and use regulations governing the placement of lights.

The 1968 "California Special" GT/CS was available only in California, and only on hardtops. About 5000 of these cars were built, with a Shelby rear deck lid, sequential tail lights, and non-functional rear scoops. Additional identifying features include the side stripe, Lucas or Marchal fog lights, and styled steel wheels.

The Mustang badge was deleted from the all-black air intake, but the interior and the engine (overleaf) were left unchanged: like the majority of "Special" Mustangs, the California Special was an exterior trim package only. Not that the standard 289 cid engine was anything to complain about....

The 1968 Mustang Shelby GT350 was a long way from the car that had originally borne the GT350 label: it was very much a road car, rather than a racer on the road. The engine was a standard production 302 cid instead of the high-performance 289 cid, though a Cobra intake manifold and Holley 600 cfm carburetor did give it 250 bhp instead of the stock 210 bhp. Even so, this was 56 bhp less than the previous year's 289 cid motor – though in all fairness, a Paxton supercharger was optional. The super-aggressive front end was again a GRP add-on. The same car appears overleaf.

A 140 mph speedo, and a rev-counter with a blood line at 6000 rpm speak for themselves. Without extensive suspension modifications, though, the blown Cobras could become excessively interesting on the corners: these cars were pretty much "straight-line specials," ideal for the traditional American demand for dragster acceleration.

Unlike modern turbos, superchargers suffer from no "lag" and deliver all of their power, all through the rev range, immediately on demand. Also, a supercharger is a much simpler and more reliable device than a turbocharger, though it is also very much less fuel efficient; a turbocharger uses exhaust gas energy that would otherwise be wasted.

The GT500KR (also overleaf) was the ultimate performance Mustang for 1968. The Cobra Jet 428 cid engine was rated at 335 bhp, but was generally reckoned to deliver closer to 400 bhp. Cobra badges were used liberally.

The Boss 302 appeared in 1969 and was powered by an up-rated version of the standard 302 cid engine delivering 290 bhp – 70 bhp more than standard. There were no fake scoops, the matte black hood reduced glare, and the rest of the matte black around the headlights and on the tail just helped it to look mean. It was one of the most functional-looking Mustangs since the original GT350, and the 302 cid engine meant that it was quite well-balanced and sweet-handling, so it was one of the nicest to drive as well. Fortunately for drivers, many people prefer the more powerful models, so Boss 302 prices can be (relatively) reasonable.

The rear window slats are particularly useful in California where they reduce interior heating from the sun. The "Boss 302" C-stripe was a styling cue taken from the GT40 racers, and it had the desired effect of making the car look longer and lower. Casting "Boss 302" into the valve covers would have looked better, though, than just using stickers.

This 1969 429 Boss (also overleaf) was powered by the 375 bhp NASCAR "homologation special" engine, and was extensively modified. A tendency to nose-heaviness meant that it required skillful driving at the limit, however; the 302 was an easier car to handle, but nothing like as fast.

BOSS 429

This 429 Boss is wonderfully threatening in a deep, rich red with a massive hood-mounted scoop. The huge powerplant had to be "shoehorned" into the engine compartment, though, and working on ancillaries can be difficult. You can see how the hood scoop works: the ram effect is not particularly important at anything like normal speeds, but what is important is that a hood scoop collects cool air, permitting a denser (and therefore more powerful) charge to be sucked into each cylinder.

Grandé, complete with the accent on the E, was the name for the top-of-the-line coupé. The vinyl roof is an identifying factor for the 1970 Grandé; so is the houndstooth upholstery. In truth, Grandés are usually among the less exciting Mustangs, and they were normally ordered with one of the "cooking" engines.

The Mach 1 Twister Special of 1970 was striking to look at, with its special paint and graphics, and this one with the 428 cid Cobra Jet ram air engine found on other Mach 1 Mustangs was a striking car to drive as well.

Cast-alloy go-faster stripes certainly look more impressive than the stick-on variety, though some found the matte-black interior to be somewhat claustrophobic. Twist-type hood latches replaced NASCAR catches in 1970.

The spoiler at the prow of the Mach 1 was not merely ornamental; with the 335 bhp engine, even the relatively unaerodynamic Mustang could be pushed along surprisingly rapidly. In place of the matte black hoods of yore, though, the hood was painted the same color as the rest of the body but with a central stripe which could be either matte black (as on this example) or white; shades of the old "up-and-over" Shelby stripe. Unlike some models, the 1970 Mustangs seemed to look as good in dark colors as in bright.

The "shaker" scoop that protruded through the hood, and shook with the engine, can clearly be seen above. This particular "styling cue" was borrowed from dragsters; it would have been equally possible, though less dramatic, to arrange for the ingress of cool air through the front grille or even via side vents. The engine itself owed most of its power to the old American saying, "You can't beat cubic inches," though more than 50 bhp/liter is not too bad for a big V8.

"All new for '70" was more than a slight exaggeration; the 1970 cars were mildly restyled compared with the major restyle of 1969. Even so, the cars were handsome enough, though replacing the outer headlights with imitation air-scoops looked suspiciously like a cost-cutting touch. The rear tail-light panel was arguably neater flat than it had been when it was concave, though the advantages of recessed tail lights are more disputable: they were quite hard to clean, and could be all but invisible when muddy.

The first generation of Mustangs – before the advent of the Mustang II – came to an end in 1973. The horsepower race was over (the most powerful engine available was the 266 bhp, 351 cid), and Ford had pretty much left the car alone for almost two years, pending the arrival of the new model.

The right car in the right place at the right time: the dramatically downsized 1974 Mustang II met the demand, sparked by the "gas crisis," for economical cars. In the main picture, low-angle photography disguises just how much smaller the Mustang II was; it does however show quite clearly how the long hood/ short deck styling cues of the previous generation were echoed in the new model. The rear treatment, with its integrated, multi-colored lights is very much more modern than the older tail-ends, while the area around the headlamps harks back to the previous generation's design and seems almost excessively styled; there are so many bends and curves in a small area of sheet metal that you immediately begin to fear moisture traps and rust. On the grille, though, the galloping pony unmistakably announces that this is a Mustang.

"Ghia," the name of the old-established coachbuilder recently acquired by Ford, was applied to the top-of-the-line Mustang II Coupé, with its fake wood dash and its glued-on pin stripes. And instead of a galloping pony, the gas cap bore a government health warning.... The first Ghias appeared in 1974; this is a 1978.

The 1978 model year saw the last of the Mustang II cars, which died largely unlamented. The $1277 King Cobra option was a cosmetic, wheels and suspension package for the top-of-the-line SportsRoof fastback equipped with the 302 cid engine (rated at a modest 134 bhp).

The styling of the King Cobra was love-it-or-hate-it. Those who loved it called it dramatic and original; those who hated it said it looked like a late 1960s record cover. Either way, both the paint and the brushed-metal dash look like period pieces today.

The 1979 Indy Pace Car Replica (also overleaf) looked much better than the 1978 King Cobra: the new body was a significantly better canvas on which to work.

Like the King Cobra, though, the Pace Car Replica was a cosmetic package, not a speed or handling package; the Old Faithful 302 cid engine now delivered 140 bhp.

The 20th Anniversary Edition Mustang of 1984 (also seen overleaf) was a fine-looking car which sported GT350 side-stripes and 1965-type side emblems; but the majority were delivered with the 5.0 liter HO engine delivering 175 bhp – an improvement over the 134 bhp days, but still a long way from the peak power of the Muscle Cars. Others came with the 4-cylinder turbo. Interior appointments were much more luxurious than in the original GT350; but you would never have been able to hear a radio or a tape deck in a properly-driven Shelby GT350. On pages 92/93 is the real performance Mustang of the mid-1980s: the grossly underrated 1984-1/2 SVO.

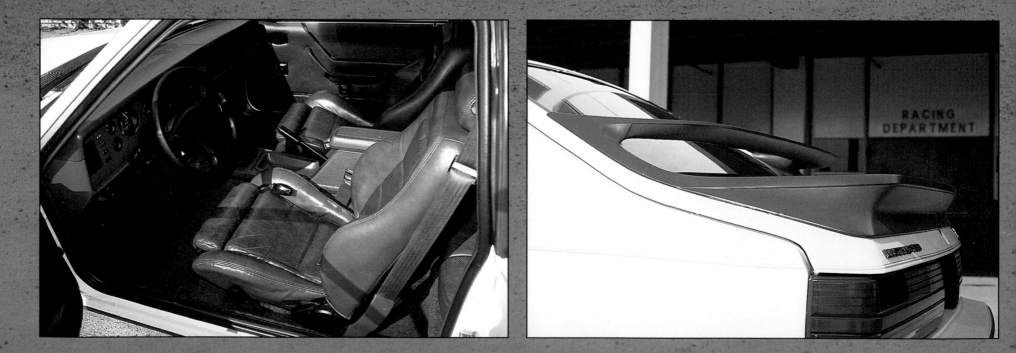

The SVO had the same 175 bhp power as the 302 cid/5 liter HO V8, but it achieved it in a completely different way: it was a turbocharged four of half the V8's capacity. The result was a relatively light, very nimble package which was however probably better suited to the European market than to American conditions: it was a car to be driven quickly and confidently on winding roads, but it was not at its best as a dragster. When fitted with the 5-liter engine it was its own biggest competitor: the V8 was much cheaper to buy, significantly easier to maintain, and considerably quicker from a standing start.

In 1987, the Mustang LX was revised to give "Euro-styled" rounded corners. The front and rear lights were both treated much more smoothly than in the previous design, reflecting changes in fashion. The previous prow had looked smart enough when it was introduced, but the new treatment suddenly made the old front look like an elderly Volvo. Genuine alloy wheels – not wheel covers, not "styled steel" wheels – were very smart indeed, and badging and decoration was commendably restrained. In fact, 1987 pretty much saw the arrival of the definitive modern Mustang.

Electronic fuel injection raised the 302 cid HO engine to 225 bhp in 1987; and remember, these are SAE net horsepower, not the old "gross" variety.

Molding "MUSTANG" into the rear bumper was very much in the spirit of the age in the late 1980s, and of course the hatchback was typical of the period.

The convertible was reintroduced to the Mustang line-up as long ago as 1983, but if you want "go" as well as "show," the Saleen Mustang is like an up-to-date (but less radical) Cobra, with plenty of "go-faster" modifications. This is a 1988 model.

In a sense, a Saleen is only "finishing the job" that Ford began, with extra-quality fittings, better wheels, a rather handsome rear spoiler, revised suspension and so forth. But the question is, would people pay Saleen's prices (which add significantly to the price of an already top-of-the-line Mustang) if they were "only" buying a Ford? After all, the SVO Mustang was a very fine piece of machinery, but the popular perception seems to have been that it was too expensive for "just" a Mustang.

Like many modern fast cars, the Saleen Mustang pays as much attention to creature comforts as to speed and handling. The days of the old-fashioned Spartan sports car are gone; today, people will put up with basic interiors only in the very cheapest cars, or (paradoxically) in the most expensive supercars like the Ferrari F40, where everything is sacrificed to lightness and speed. The Saleen is also shown overleaf; note the "302" badge – cubic inches instead of liters.

This is The Car That Wouldn't Die. The old 302 cid engine has been renamed 5.0 "liter" and delivers 225 bhp – not much less than the 290 bhp version in the Boss 302, given the difference between SAE gross and SAE nett – but in a lighter, better-handling car.

You could not call the exterior styling of the current GT particularly inspired, but the view from inside the car is something else altogether. The electrically adjustable seats are far more comfortable than on earlier models and offer better support; the five-speed gearbox knocks the old three-speed "crash" 'box into a cocked hat; there is cruise control; there is air conditioning; there is lots of space under the hatch. The car is more economical, and handles significantly better. The only question is, how much do we care for practicality, and how much for style?

This is a 1989 convertible, though you would have to look very hard indeed to distinguish it from a significantly newer car: changes since then have been minor and evolutionary, and mostly involve getting more power from the four-cylinder engine. The basic ragtop may lack the elegance of the Saleen conversion, but it is still a very attractive car.

The modern Mustang Convertible (also shown overleaf) is about as affordable as a convertible gets today (and remember, it's supposed to be a personal car, not a practical family car), and surely that is what Mustangs are about: affordable, reliable, comfortable fun.